M.V. MILAN

SELLING 101

The Ultimate Guide to Best Selling Techniques,
Discover Effective Strategies on How To Make
Even an Unknown Product Be a Bestseller

Descrierea CIP a Bibliotecii Naţionale a României
M.V. MILAN
   SELLING 101. The Ultimate Guide to Best Selling
Techniques, Discover Effective Strategies on How To Make
Even an Unknown Product Be a Bestseller / M.V. Milan –
Bucharest: Editura My Ebook, 2020
   ISBN

M.V. MILAN

SELLING 101

**The Ultimate Guide to Best Selling Techniques,
Discover Effective Strategies on How To Make
Even an Unknown Product Be a Bestseller**

My Ebook Publishing House
Bucharest, 2020

TABLE OF CONTENTS

INTRODUCTION

If you want to make big sales online you need to have at least one best selling product that constantly sells well for you. The ideal situation would of course be to have several best selling products... but that part comes later.

First you have to start with one product, and that's what we'll be looking at in this report. Once you have that, it's a case of repeating that success in the future and building your business from there.

So let's go through this step by step and see how it can be done.

WHAT TYPE OF PRODUCT SHOULD YOU SELL?

We're not talking about the specific product here; we're talking about what form the product takes. This is important because it can have a real effect on how you handle those sales once they start coming in.

So let's see the two basic types of product you have to choose from:

TANGIBLE PRODUCTS

Tangible means something that you can touch, so for our purposes this would be anything that would need to be sent through the mail. From DVDs to gadgets, anything that you can put into a Jiffy bag and mail to your customer is a tangible product.

The advantage with these is that you have an actual physical product to sell, but the disadvantage is that there are a lot more risks to take with them. Supposing you take in some stock of a product that isn't selling at the moment in the hope of turning it into a best seller… and it doesn't sell? You're left with plenty of stock taking up space, and you've lost money as a result.

There is a better way if you want to go the tangible goods route – and in fact there are two options for you here.

Firstly you could become an affiliate marketer and refer other people to tangible products sold by a third party. This means you refer the sale, you get a percentage of that sale for your efforts, and the third party that stocks the product takes care of the physical process of sending it out to the customer.

Your second option is to get into dropshipping. This is a similar process but the difference is normally that while the company processes the order and sends it to the customer, it is often sent so it looks as if it came directly from you.

The other difference is that the customer places the order with you, and you then place the order – having taken your commission off first – with the customer's information added in as the delivery details.

This obviously involves more work but you will get your commission up front and therefore you won't need to wait until you reach the commission payout level that is set by the site you are using for your affiliate products.

INTANGIBLE PRODUCTS

Intangible means something that cannot be touched. For our purposes here that points directly to products which need to be downloaded. This can include reports, newsletters, eBooks and even some items of software or applications.

Now the advantages of these are very clear – first of all they are all based on information, so if you want to create your own product from scratch it is far easier to do it with an intangible and downloadable product than it is to do it any other way.

Secondly you will have the advantage of offering the product instantly. The customer gets access to their copy the second they have paid for it; no waiting for a few days to receive it in the mail. This is a big selling feature and worth bearing in mind.

Thirdly there is a lot less risk in taking on (or creating) an intangible product because you don't have to shell out any cash to stock it in the first place. If it doesn't sell you don't lose anything and you aren't left with that huge and worrying pile of stock.

A lot of people start off by promoting other people's downloadable products as affiliates, and then branch off into creating their own once they have explored the market a bit and have more knowledge of how to do it.

So those are your options. Let's now look at the next step.

IDENTIFYING AN UNKNOWN PRODUCT

This begs one big question – how do you find something that no one knows about?

It's a worthy question, but if you know how to answer it you'll be much more likely to find and promote the products that no one else has found yet.

Now for a product to be unknown, that clearly points to the fact that it exists already, so it won't include anything you come up with yourself. We will touch on this later on though so if you do have ideas you'll get to know more in a while.

The only completely unknown product that you will ever come across is one that is brand new and about to launch. It IS possible to find out about these if you move in the right circles though, and the best way to become a promoter of this type of product is to subscribe to plenty of email newsletters by some of the biggest names in internet marketing. These people know the power of getting an army of affiliates to help them launch their new products for them, so you can get in on the ground floor on plenty of occasions here.

The other type of unknown product is one that has been around for a while and just not taken off. When you think about a best seller, you will think of something that EVERYONE knows about, whether they have one or not.

Think of JK Rowling's Harry Potter books, for example, or the DVD of "Titanic", or any one of hundreds of other products. Even if you don't have it yourself you will know people who do.

What we're trying to do here is to turn a product that hasn't made many sales into one that everyone has heard of. That's how you get a best seller – and the cash that goes with it.

WHERE TO LOOK

We've already mentioned the fact that hooking up with well known internet marketers will result in being one of the first to promote new products. But if affiliate marketing is your thing then you should also join Internet sites such as JVZoo.com, ClickBank and Commission Junction – they're well known and highly respected sites which give you access to thousands and thousands of products to promote. They are free to join, but it's also worth searching on Google to find other affiliate programs in your own country.

What you need to find is something that you know isn't being widely promoted already by other people. That's why these sites are ideal for searching – because they have so many products that you can easily go off the beaten track to find just what you want.

MAKING SURE YOU PICK THE RIGHT PRODUCT

This skill will come with experience and knowledge, but your basic task here is to find something that there is a market for. Just because a product has been out for a while and hasn't sold well, that doesn't mean it's a bad product. It could just be that the people selling it haven't managed to connect with their target market very well – and if you can be an affiliate for that product you could be the one to turn things around.

IDENTIFYING THE RIGHT AUDIENCE

This should be done in conjunction with picking the right product. You can start at either end of the process in actual fact – you might find a particular type of product that you think could be a good seller in this way, or you might find a particular niche or group of people that clearly have money to spend, and then go off in search of a product that will meet their needs.

If you find a product you think will be good, you will then need to identify the potential audience for that product and ask yourself some questions to figure out whether it's a good bet to start promoting or not. Here are the kinds of things you need to be asking yourself:

- Does this audience represent a good niche market that can easily be reached online?

- Does this audience have money to spend?

- Is the product you are thinking of promoting significantly different from anything else they have seen?

- Does the product fit into the type of price they might pay?

These questions will help you to figure out whether you have chosen a good product for starters. For example, you may have found a product that is priced at $100, and is aimed at young mothers with kids. Now this could be a really good product that works and has been clearly thought out.

But you need to think about whether young mums have that kind of money to spend. Is that why this product hasn't become a best seller before now? It could well be.

HOW MANY PEOPLE COULD YOU
SELL THIS TO?

It's important to think about how big the niche is that you are thinking of targeting. Niche markets are potential money makers, but you need to make sure you don't target a niche that is so small you will exhaust it in no time.

This is a fine balance that you need to get right when marketing online, because targeting too big an audience will mean that appealing to everyone is virtually impossible, whereas going too far in the other direction will mean you have too few people to try and find.

Here's an example – targeting people who buy groceries would include virtually everyone on the planet. Targeting people who buy a specific brand of washing powder on a Thursday every week would target too few. But targeting people who are looking for an eco-friendly product to wash their clothes with might just achieve the right balance.

Remember that while you need to do your research to make sure you stand the best chance of turning an unknown product into a best seller, you also have to have a little faith and simply try it out and see what happens once you reach a certain stage in your research.

FINDING A PRODUCT FOR YOUR NICHE

If you started the other way round and found a good niche market before finding a product that would suit them, all you need to do is visit JVZoo, ClickBank or Commission Junction, or any one of the other similar sites out there on the internet today, and search for a product that would suit those customers.

You can use keywords to make this part of the process easier; think about the type of products that may suit these people and start your search there. For example, let's say you want to find a product that would appeal to people who have an interest in staying slim. You could look up health foods, slimming books, low calorie recipes, fitness, and so on. These will give you a good start, and as you find specific products that you think might fit the bill, you can move on from there.

If you are working in this way you might find it helpful to have a shortlist of products that are new to you. You can then look them up on the Internet and see whether there is a lot of links to them, any news, or much interest in them at all. You'll soon discover whether you have found an unknown product or not.

DISCOVERING A NICHE TO TARGET WITH A PRODUCT OF YOUR OWN

Everyone wants information – and it's what the internet does best. Many websites exist simply to provide information and nothing else, so it's worth considering whether you could create your own information product that will be completely unknown and never seen before.

If you come across a niche that you like the look of and you spot a gap in the market for an information product that you think you can provide, start working on your idea immediately! It's not as difficult as some people think to be able to create something like an eBook or a mini report like this one, and it could make all the difference to your income.

CONNECTING WITH YOUR AUDIENCE ONLINE

Okay, so by the time you reach this stage you will have a product to sell, and an audience to sell it to.

All you need to do now is to find out where that audience is likely to be online, and make sure that your product is going to be put right in front of them.

So how do you do this? Well, there are two main ways to succeed here:

- You find out where these people hang out and go to them

- You create a site or a web page and draw them to you

To get the best results and the best sales that you can, you should definitely try to put both of these methods into action. But the most important thing to remember is that you need to look on this as a long term thing. A failure to do this is quite often the reason that some products don't sell anywhere near as well as they should or could in the first place! It would be wonderful if you started promoting your product and found that you got fantastic sales right from day one, but that probably won't happen in all honesty. It can take a while to advertise something that eventually becomes a best seller.

So let's look at each of these methods in turn, and see how we can use them to start promoting – and selling – the item you have in mind.

GO TO YOUR AUDIENCE

In order for this to work, you need to know where to go – and one of the best places to start is to look for forums on the relevant subject.

Incidentally if you are completely stuck for ideas for products but you have a niche in mind that you want to approach, look for a forum on that subject and see what the members are talking about. It's a great way to get in touch with that niche and what makes it tick!

Now you need to be extremely careful when you are introducing a product to your audience in this way, because if you don't do it right you can get accused of spam and banned from that forum – plus it will obviously get you a bad name. That's obviously not what we're after here, so the first step is to read through the terms and conditions laid down by each individual forum you come across to see how it works.

Another good idea is to spend some time just browsing through the posts that other people have already started, so that you can get a feel for how the forum operates and the type of subjects that are covered.

You will usually find that you can link to an outside site via your signature link at the end of each post you make (this is put on automatically once you have set it up to appear), but not all forums allow this to be promotional. Again, make sure you check the rules before doing it. Quite often it is more the issue of promoting products or services during the post itself rather than in your signature that causes problems, especially if you continually do it when there is clearly no real cause (other than a promotional one) to do so.

You can also reach your audience in other ways, and with the interactive ways that many websites are operating in these days you will find this extremely easy to do.

Take MySpace for example. It doesn't take long to set up a user profile on this site and you can search for other people on the site who have the same interests as you.

The same thing applies to other similar sites such as Facebook.

These sites do take time to develop a presence on of course, so if you are looking for a faster way to attract the attention of people who are going to be interested in your product, give Twitter a go. The benefit of this is that you only have a few words in which to get your message across – and it takes very little effort to start building up a body of fans who will be interested in what you have to say.

Just remember that to get the best effect you should do more than just advertise. People will get bored very quickly if you do nothing other than point them to the product (or products) that you are advertising. Give them something worthwhile and tell them of your own interest in the subject area; if you can tell them something they don't already know that relates to the product in question then you will certainly have their attention.

You can also connect with your audience in other ways; remember that the more methods you can find for reaching the people who are likely to buy your product, the more sales you will make.

Think about using classified adverts on various websites for example. You can easily find these by searching for classified ad sites on the big search engines; some of them will be free whereas others may require a payment, but you can start with all the free methods to begin with.

One other way to connect with the people you want to sell to is by writing articles on subjects that they will be looking for. By finding out as much as you can about their interests, you will be able to get plenty of ideas on topics to write about that will attract their attention.

Your goal here is to think about what these people will be searching for online. You can then write some articles that are carefully enhanced with selected keywords and submit them to a range of article directories online. Each article will have its own unique URL, and if you write it well and make good use of the keywords without overdoing it, you will find that your articles will come up ranked quite highly in the search results your potential customers are coming up with.

That means there is a great chance of them finding your article, reading it, and then going through to the website which has details of the product you want to sell.

The key to success is to remember not to promote anything in the article. This sounds bizarre, I know, but that's how it works. And it really does work. What happens is that you get a small box at the foot of every article you write which allows you to link to a website that you have an interest in. This doesn't need to be your own website – it could just as easily be a website that you are an affiliate for.

But just as you did with the forums, make sure here too that you read all the terms and conditions about the sites that you can link to, as some won't let you link up with affiliate links. It's easy to get around though, because all you would have to do is set up your own website or blog and link to that instead.

The trick that you must remember with all of these methods is that you won't be able to turn a product into a best seller unless you push it and promote it as hard as you can. The internet is a huge place, so not only do you have to have the right audience and the right product, you also have to have the determination to get that product out there and promote it as hard and as much as you can. You won't get very far with half a dozen ads and a couple of posts on Twitter, so make sure you are ready for the long haul.

LET YOUR AUDIENCE COME TO YOU

This is very much like setting up shop in a prime location and waiting for people to come flooding through the doors.

There are two main options available to you here, and we'll look at each one in turn. Although of course, if you really want to push for that best seller, you should be doing both together! Aim big and keep aiming if you want that best selling product to be known all over the Internet.

The first option is to set up a dedicated website on the subject your niche product is concerned with. This will work especially well if you manage to track down several products in the same niche that are presently unknown, and you want to turn them all into best sellers.

Now obviously this will again work best if you don't go directly for the big sale. It's almost like a reverse psychology –

people don't like a hard sell and if you try and talk them into buying something before they are ready you will lose potential customers.

The best bet is to think about developing a useful website that will provide people with plenty of information on the relevant subject. You can then almost casually recommend the product you have in mind to sell to them.

Let's look at an example of how this works. Let's suppose you have found a 'green' product of some kind that has a benefit for the environment as well as for the consumer.

Now this could really take off because of the way that the news and the world as a whole has picked up on this topic.

But instead of just saying, "Hey look, I've found this great new product that will do this and that and save on energy every time you use it," you should instead build up a website that virtually pre-sells this and other green products to the consumer.

Think of it like this. When someone goes onto a search engine and looks for information on something they may not necessarily be looking to buy something. So if you try and sell them something the minute they arrive on your website, they are probably going to go elsewhere.

But consider this. Let's say they want to find out more about green issues and about how they can improve their lives by doing more things that will benefit the environment instead of polluting it. They aren't looking for anything in particular to buy, but they might just be persuaded if they find out about something that could help them.

So your job is to make sure that you give them all the information and insight they are looking for, before gently introducing them to the products that you want to sell.

It's quite often the quality of this pre-selling phase that turns a reasonable seller into a best seller. You can introduce them to your product via your affiliate link in many different ways, but the route to getting there should always be the same in that you should make every effort to give your customer the best information and the best advice before you actually try and close out the sale.

It's obvious that you will need to get as much qualified traffic coming to your website as possible if you are going to turn your unknown products into best sellers. You could get a reasonably high visitor to order ratio... but if you only get a dozen or so visitors a week then you won't get the sales and the income you want.

Okay so that's your website underway – now what about a blog?

Blogs are great for transforming an average product into an outstanding one, because you get to be a little more personal and approachable for your visitors. A website has its purpose and its place in things, but it has a habit of standing in between you and your customers.

A blog, on the other hand, is very different. A blog is more personal. It's more intimate in a sense, because you are talking directly to the people who are reading your entries. Each blog post is an address from you to them, and this has a distinct advantage.

What you will be doing is building a relationship with your readers as your blog goes from being just a few posts in length to several, and then builds into many different sections. So long as you keep it on topic you will find that some people will find you and keep coming back to see what else you have to say on your chosen topic (or niche). This points out exactly why you need to be interested in your subject, because in this example you could be writing about it for a long time to come. And if you love your niche then other people will be pulled in by it and will be much more likely to buy from you as a result.

THE WORD OF MOUTH RULE

One big aspect of any product becoming a best seller is the fact that other people do some of the advertising and promotion for you, without you asking them to.

If you think about this you will find that it's true. If you buy a product that you are delighted with and you absolutely love – no matter what it is – you will find that you start to tell other people about it. And there is every chance that some of those people will buy the product and repeat the process by telling people that they know about it too. In some cases they may even hop online and go on a forum or even their own blog and tell the world about it, helpfully providing a link to the place they got the information from in the first place.

This is the pinnacle of success as far as any marketer is concerned. If you can get people talking about your product then you will make more sales without even trying. This is why I mentioned the prospect of getting in touch with your audience – your potential customers – via social networking websites such as Facebook, because if they like what you have to offer then there is every chance of you being able to make more sales and get your 'unknown' product promoted on a much wider scale.

So don't discount the power of word of mouth, because this could provide the final push that turns a regular product into one that can't keep up with demand.

PULLING IT ALL TOGETHER

So we have now seen the entire process of selling something that very few people – if anyone – have seen before. Depending on how good you are at getting used to this process, you may strike it lucky and research and find an ideal product on your first attempt.

But if that doesn't happen, don't worry. It doesn't mean you won't be able to turn an unknown product into a best seller, it just means that it may take more than one attempt to find the right product.

But whatever product you settle on – whether it is one of your own or something that someone else has created – it is absolutely vital to keep going with your advertising and promoting efforts long term. You really need to approach this with a determined and focused effort.

So if you start off by building and launching a website to promote your products as we discussed before, move on to create a blog to run alongside it. Make the effort to look for plenty of sites to put some classified adverts on. Make sure you get yourself onto some of the social networking sites and start linking up with other people who are interested in the same kind of thing.

I cannot stress how important it is to really go for broke – figuratively speaking – when you want to take an unknown product and make a mint from it. Because of that I would suggest that you read this report through from start to finish several times before you actually set about finding that first product. It will ensure that you understand each and every step and you know exactly what you will need to do next.

The good news is that this process becomes more familiar as you go along, so don't give up! You'll also get better at spotting what is more likely to qualify as a best seller, so even if you don't hit the jackpot the first time round, your chances will get better and better with each attempt.

And who knows, I could soon be writing another report using YOUR success story as an example of how to do it!

Good luck – and remember that the best time to get started is NOW.

9 786069 837184

Printed by Libri Plureos GmbH in Hamburg,
Germany